My Mother's Life Story

A window into my mother's heart

Cheryl Pryor

Arlington & Amelia

Arlington & Amelia Publishers

ArlingtonAmeliaPub@cfl.rr.com

First Printing

ISBN:10-1-886541-26-4
ISBN:13-978-1-886541-2-69

FOR

MY MOTHER

JOYCE NEWHOUSE - BRACKETT

TABLE OF CONTENTS

About This Book

ABOUT THIS BOOK

While mom is a prominent figure in our life growing up, it is usually not until our later years that we really appreciate what an important part she played in our life. Not only did she give us life, but she helped mold our character and had a big impact on who we are as an adult.

Many times we never think of her as a child or of having had a life before us as her children. We have become so consumed with our own lives that we rarely take the time to really find out about mom and her life, both before we were around and now that the nest is empty.

My Mother's Life Story' is one of the most in-depth journals about a mother's life you will find. Get to really know your mother by having her fill this book out for you. You will be able to see who she is as a complete person. You will treasure it in days to come, if for no other reason than to have the information to pass on to your own children.

Perhaps this is a book mom has purchased herself and filled out and given to you as a gift. If so, be thankful she took the time to do so. It is a window into her thoughts, her dreams, her heart.

One day she won't be here to answer those questions and if you don't get the answers now, they will be lost forever.

'My *Mother's Life Story'* is in-depth and there may be questions that don't apply to some and some that may be a little too painful to answer – the questions that don't apply or which she would prefer not to answer she can choose to skip, as this is her journal, her life story.

You will be guaranteed to learn something you never knew before or would have never thought to ask. Enjoy getting to know your mother through 'My *Mother's Life Story: A window into my mother's heart.'*

This book is for my child (Name) _____

Written by _____

Year written _____

My age at the time this was written _____

Personal message to my child:

_____

_____

_____

_____

_____

_____

1

VITAL STATISTICS

YOUR FULL NAME (INCLUDING YOUR MAIDEN NAME)

_____

NAME YOU GO BY

_____

PLACE OF BIRTH

_____

DATE OF BIRTH

_____

PARENTS FULL NAMES

MOTHERS _____

FATHERS _____

2

AT THE TIME I WAS BORN

WHO WAS PRESIDENT AT THE TIME OF YOUR BIRTH

_____

CURRENT EVENTS AT THE TIME OF YOUR BIRTH

_____

_____

_____

_____

_____

AT THE TIME OF MY BIRTH, THE AVERAGE COST OF:

A HOME _____

A CAR _____

GAS _____

A LOAF OF BREAD _____

3

MY YOUTH

NAME OF HOSPITAL WHERE YOU WERE BORN

_____

CITY & STATE WHERE YOU WERE BORN

_____

WHAT IS YOUR FIRST MEMORY

_____

_____

_____

_____

_____

IN YOUR YOUTH WAS THERE ANYONE WHO WAS A PART OF YOUR LIFE
THAT YOU HAVE FOND MEMORIES OF

_____

FAVORITES AS A CHILD:

TOY _____

_____

_____

GAMES YOU PLAYED _____

_____

_____

TV SHOWS _____

_____

_____

FRIENDS _____

_____

_____

ANYTHING ADDITIONAL YOU WOULD LIKE TO ADD

_____

_____

_____

_____

4

CHILDHOOD DAYS

FAVORITE FOODS AS A CHILD

_____

_____

_____

FOODS YOU DID NOT LIKE AS A CHILD

_____

_____

_____

AS A CHILD DID YOU SPEND MOST OF YOUR LEISURE TIME INDOORS OR OUTDOORS

_____

_____

_____

WOULD YOU DESCRIBE YOUR FAMILY WHILE GROWING UP AS

VERY RICH   *RICH*   *WELL OFF*   *MIDDLE CLASS*

GETTING BY   *POOR*   *DESTITUTE*   _____

HARDSHIPS YOU SUFFERED WHILE GROWING UP

_____

_____

_____

_____

_____

_____

_____

WHAT ARE YOU MOST THANKFUL FOR FROM THE DAYS OF YOUR CHILDHOOD

_____

_____

_____

_____

_____

DESCRIBE THE RELATIONSHIP YOU HAD WITH YOUR:

PARENTS _____

_____

_____

_____

SIBLINGS _____

_____

_____

_____

GRANDPARENTS: MATERNAL _____

_____

_____

_____

GRANDPARENTS: PATERNAL _____

_____

_____

_____

WHAT WAS YOUR BEDROOM LIKE AS A CHILD

_____

_____

_____

_____

WHAT WAS YOUR MOST PRIZED POSSESSION

_____

_____

_____

DID YOU HAVE A NICKNAME WHILE YOU WERE GROWING UP
IF SO, WHO GAVE IT TO YOU AND WHY

_____

_____

_____

_____

WHILE GROWING UP WERE YOU INVOLVED IN:

GIRL SCOUTS _____

_____

ANY CLUBS OR ORGANIZATIONS _____

_____

FRIENDS YOU HAD WHILE GROWING UP

_____

_____

_____

_____

_____

BEST FRIENDS

_____

_____

_____

_____

_____

WHO WAS YOUR FIRST CRUSH; DID HE KNOW; AGE AT THE TIME

_____

_____

_____

_____

VACATIONS YOU WENT ON AS A FAMILY

_____

_____

_____

_____

_____

_____

_____

YOUR MOST MEMORABLE VACATION AS A CHILD & WHY IT WAS SPECIAL

_____

_____

_____

_____

_____

_____

_____

_____

INVENTIONS OR TECHNOLOGY OF TODAY THAT DIDN'T EXIST DURING YOUR CHILDHOOD

_____

_____

_____

_____

_____

_____

_____

_____

_____

_____

_____

_____

_____

_____

_____

5

TEEN YEARS

POPULAR TRENDS, STYLES, OR TYPE OF MUSIC THAT WAS POPULAR WHILE YOU WERE GROWING UP

_____

_____

_____

WHAT TYPE OF MUSIC DID YOU LISTEN TO AS A TEEN

_____

_____

_____

CONCERTS YOU WENT TO

_____

_____

_____

WHAT ARE SOME THINGS THAT ARE DIFFERENT NOW FROM WHEN YOU WERE GROWING UP

_____

_____

_____

_____

_____

_____

_____

_____

_____

_____

WHILE GROWING UP WERE YOU INVOLVED IN:

MUSIC _____

_____

SPORTS _____

_____

DANCE _____

OTHER _____

_____

HOBBIES YOU HAD WHILE GROWING UP

_____

_____

_____

INTERESTS YOU HAD WHILE GROWING UP

_____

_____

_____

HOW DID YOU SPEND YOUR LEISURE TIME: AFTER SCHOOL & WEEKENDS

_____

_____

_____

_____

AT WHAT AGE DID YOU BEGIN TO DATE

_____

_____

WHERE DID YOU GO ON YOUR FIRST DATE

_____

_____

_____

WHO WAS YOUR FIRST SERIOUS BOYFRIEND

_____

_____

_____

OTHER BOYFRIENDS

_____

_____

_____

_____

_____

WHO TAUGHT YOU HOW TO DRIVE

_____

AT WHAT AGE

_____

MEMORIES OF LEARNING TO DRIVE

_____

_____

_____

_____

_____

MEMORY OF GETTING YOUR FIRST DRIVER'S LICENSE

_____

_____

_____

_____

_____

_____

WHERE DID YOU ATTEND HIGH SCHOOL (INCLUDE CITY & STATE)

_____

_____

_____

WHAT WERE YOUR FAVORITE SUBJECTS YOU STUDIED IN HIGH SCHOOL

_____

_____

_____

_____

WHAT YEAR DID YOU GRADUATE FROM HIGH SCHOOL

_____

DESCRIBE YOUR GRADUATION

_____

_____

_____

_____

_____

_____

WHAT DID YOU DO ON "GRAD NIGHT"

_____

_____

_____

_____

_____

_____

WHAT WAS YOUR FIRST CAR: MAKE, MODEL, YEAR

_____

_____

HOW MUCH DID YOU PAY FOR THE CAR, AMOUNT OF MONTHLY PAYMENTS

_____

_____

_____

HOW OLD WERE YOU WHEN YOU GOT YOUR FIRST CAR

_____

_____

6

EDUCATION

WHERE DID YOU ATTEND SCHOOL:

KINDERGARTEN _____

ELEMENTARY SCHOOL _____

_____

_____

_____

MIDDLE SCHOOL _____

_____

_____

_____

HIGH SCHOOL _____

_____

_____

_____

COLLEGE _____

_____

_____

_____

MAJORED IN

_____

_____

_____

DID YOU BELONG TO A SORORITY

_____

_____

MEMORABLE EVENTS FROM COLLEGE DAYS

_____

_____

_____

_____

DEGREE

_____

_____

_____

YEAR GRADUATED

_____

ANYTHING ADDITIONAL YOU WOULD LIKE TO ADD

_____

_____

_____

_____

_____

_____

_____

_____

_____

_____

7

SIBLINGS

NAMES OF YOUR SIBLINGS IN BIRTH ORDER & THEIR BIRTHDATES

_____

_____

_____

_____

_____

DESCRIBE YOUR SIBLINGS AS THEY WERE GROWING UP

_____

_____

_____

_____

_____

_____

_____

WHICH OF YOUR SIBLINGS WERE YOU CLOSEST TO WHILE GROWING UP

_____

_____

SPECIAL MEMORIES

_____

_____

_____

_____

_____

_____

_____

_____

ANYTHING ADDITIONAL YOU WOULD LIKE TO ADD

_____

_____

_____

_____

_____

8

PLACES I'VE LIVED

DESCRIBE THE NEIGHBORHOOD YOU GREW UP IN

MY FAVORITE PLACE I LIVED WHILE GROWING UP & WHY

_____

_____

_____

_____

_____

_____

_____

_____

_____

NAME ALL THE PLACES YOU LIVED FROM YOUR BIRTH TO THE CURRENT TIME (INCLUDE ADDRESSES IF YOU REMEMBER)

_____

_____

_____

_____

_____

_____

_____

_____

_____

_____

ANYTHING ADDITIONAL YOU WOULD LIKE TO ADD

_____

_____

_____

_____

_____

_____

_____

_____

_____

_____

_____

9

FAMILY LIFE

TRADITIONS IN OUR FAMILY WE HAD WHILE GROWING UP

_____

_____

_____

_____

_____

_____

_____

_____

_____

_____

AS A FAMILY DID YOU GO TO:

SPORTING EVENTS, CAMPING, HIKING, MOVIES, OR OTHER EVENTS

_____

_____

_____

_____

_____

AS A FAMILY DID YOU PARTICIPATE IN:

SWIMMING, BOATING, WATER SKIING, SNOW SKIING, BIKING, PLAY TENNIS, GOLF, OTHER SPORTING ACTIVITIES

_____

_____

_____

_____

_____

OTHER ACTIVITIES YOU DID AS A FAMILY OR ON YOUR OWN WHILE GROWING UP

_____

_____

_____

_____

_____

SOME OF YOUR HAPPIEST MOMENTS WHILE GROWING UP

_____

_____

_____

_____

_____

_____

_____

_____

_____

_____

SOME OF YOUR SADDEST MOMENTS WHILE GROWING UP

_____

_____

_____

_____

_____

_____

_____

_____

_____

_____

_____

AS A FAMILY DID YOU ATTEND CHURCH, SYNAGOGUE, OR OTHER RELIGIOUS ORGANIZATIONS

_____

_____

DENOMINATION

_____

_____

BAPTISM, COMMUNION, BAT MITZVAH, OTHER

_____

_____

HOW DO YOU THINK CHILDREN DIFFER TODAY FROM THE ERA YOU GREW UP IN

_____

_____

_____

_____

_____

_____

_____

_____

HOW DO PARENTS IN GENERAL TODAY DIFFER FROM THE ERA YOU GREW UP IN

_____

_____

_____

_____

_____

_____

_____

10

HOLIDAYS & VACATIONS

WHAT WAS YOUR FAVORITE HOLIDAY AS A CHILD

_____

_____

_____

_____

_____

IS IT STILL YOUR FAVORITE HOLIDAY TODAY

_____

_____

_____

_____

_____

_____

_____

_____

HOW WERE HOLIDAYS IN MY CHILDHOOD CELEBRATED

NEW YEAR'S EVE

_____

_____

_____

_____

VALENTINE'S DAY

_____

_____

_____

_____

EASTER

_____

_____

_____

_____

_____

_____

_____

MEMORIAL DAY

_____

_____

_____

_____

INDEPENDENCE DAY OR 4TH OF JULY

_____

_____

_____

_____

LABOR DAY

_____

_____

_____

_____

HALLOWEEN

_____

_____

_____

_____

_____

_____

_____

THANKSGIVING

_____

_____

_____

_____

_____

CHANUKAH OR HANUKKAH

_____

_____

_____

_____

CHRISTMAS

_____

_____

_____

_____

_____

_____

_____

OTHER HOLIDAYS YOUR FAMILY MAY HAVE CELEBRATED

_____

_____

_____

_____

BIRTHDAYS

_____

_____

_____

_____

_____

_____

_____

SPECIAL BIRTHDAY MEMORIES

_____

_____

_____

_____

_____

_____

_____

11

PETS THROUGH THE YEARS

PETS YOU HAD WHILE GROWING UP

12

PEOPLE OF INFLUENCE

WHO IS THE PERSON WHO MOST INFLUENCED YOU

_____

_____

IN WHAT WAY

_____

_____

_____

_____

PEOPLE I MET GROWING UP I'LL NEVER FORGET

_____

_____

_____

13

MY PARENTS – YOUR GRANDPARENTS

MOTHER'S NAME INCLUDING MAIDEN NAME

_____

YOUR MOTHER'S BIRTHDATE

_____

YOUR MOTHER'S PLACE OF BIRTH

_____

YOUR MOTHER'S SIBLINGS

_____

_____

_____

_____

_____

_____

WHERE DID YOUR MOTHER GROW UP (CITY, STATE)

_____

FATHER'S NAME

_____

YOUR FATHER'S BIRTHDATE

_____

YOUR FATHER'S PLACE OF BIRTH

_____

YOUR FATHER'S SIBLINGS

_____

_____

_____

_____

_____

_____

WHERE DID YOUR FATHER GROW UP (CITY, STATE)

_____

WHERE DID YOUR PARENTS MEET

_____

_____

_____

_____

WHERE YOUR PARENTS WERE MARRIED

_____

_____

NAME OF THE CHURCH WHERE THEY MARRIED

_____

_____

_____

AGES WHEN MARRIED

MOTHER _____

FATHER _____

AGE & CAUSE OF DEATH:

MOTHER _____

FATHER _____

LOCATION OF BURIAL

MOTHER _____

FATHER _____

YEARS OF EDUCATION

MOTHER _____

FATHER _____

HARDSHIPS THEY EXPERIENCED GROWING UP

MOTHER _____

_____

_____

_____

_____

FATHER _____

_____

_____

_____

_____

HOW ARE TIMES DIFFERENT TODAY THAN WHEN YOUR PARENTS WERE GROWING UP

_____

_____

_____

_____

_____

_____

_____

_____

WERE YOUR PARENTS MARRIED OR DIVORCED FOR MOST OF YOUR CHILDHOOD

_____

_____

_____

IF DIVORCED, WHO DID YOU LIVE WITH

_____

_____

_____

IF DIVORCED, WAS THE PARENT YOU DIDN'T LIVE WITH A PART OF YOUR LIFE

_____

_____

_____

_____

DID YOU HAVE A STEPFATHER

_____

IF YOU HAD A STEPFATHER, WAS HE AN INFLUENCE IN YOUR LIFE
IF SO, IN WHAT WAY

_____

_____

_____

_____

_____

_____

_____

_____

MEMORIES OF MY PARENTS

MOTHER

_____

_____

_____

_____

_____

_____

_____

FATHER

_____

_____

_____

_____

_____

_____

_____

WHAT WERE YOUR PARENT'S OCCUPATIONS & WHERE DID THEY WORK

MOTHER

_____

_____

_____

_____

_____

FATHER

_____

_____

_____

_____

_____

WHAT I MOST ADMIRED ABOUT MY PARENTS

MOTHER

_____

_____

_____

_____

_____

_____

FATHER

_____

_____

_____

_____

_____

IF YOU CAME FROM A DYSFUNCTIONAL FAMILY, ANY COMMENTS YOU
WANT TO SHARE

_____

_____

_____

_____

_____

IS THERE A SPECIAL GIFT YOU RECEIVED AT ANY TIME FROM YOUR PARENTS THAT MEANT A LOT TO YOU

_____

_____

_____

_____

_____

LOOKING BACK NOW THAT _____
HAS PASSED AWAY, I WISH...

_____

_____

_____

_____

_____

_____

_____

_____

14

MY GRANDPARENTS – YOUR GREAT GRANDPARENTS

WHAT DO YOU REMEMBER ABOUT YOUR GRANDPARENTS

MY MOTHER'S PARENTS

_____

_____

_____

_____

_____

_____

_____

_____

_____

MY FATHER'S PARENTS

_____

_____

_____

_____

_____

_____

_____

_____

_____

GRANDPARENTS NAMES & BIRTHPLACE

MY MOTHER'S PARENTS

_____

_____

_____

_____

_____

MY FATHER'S PARENTS

_____

_____

_____

_____

_____

GRANDPARENTS OCCUPATIONS

MY MOTHER'S PARENTS

_____

_____

_____

_____

_____

MY FATHER'S PARENTS

_____

_____

_____

_____

_____

_____

WAS THERE ANYTHING THEY PASSED ON TO YOU OR A GIFT THEY GAVE YOU THAT MEANT A LOT TO YOU

_____

_____

_____

_____

_____

WAS THERE ANYTHING THEY TAUGHT YOU THAT HAS STUCK WITH YOU THROUGH THE YEARS

_____

_____

_____

_____

_____

15

OUR HERITAGE – OUR ANCESTORS

EVEN THOUGH THIS IS THE LIFE STORY OF YOUR MOTHER, OUR ANCESTORS AND THEIR CHARACTER AND WHY THEY MADE THE DECISIONS THEY DID HAVE AN AFFECT ON OUR OWN LIVES. HER ANCESTORS, WHETHER SHE KNEW THEM OR NOT, ARE A PART OF HER LIFE STORY.

WHAT IS THE NATIONALITY OF YOUR ANCESTORS

MATERNAL

_____

_____

_____

PATERNAL

_____

_____

_____

DO YOU HAVE ANY INFORMATION ON YOUR GREAT-GRANDPARENTS

MATERNAL

_____

_____

_____

_____

_____

PATERNAL

_____

_____

_____

_____

_____

DO YOU KNOW ANY OF YOUR ANCESTOR'S OCCUPATIONS

MATERNAL:

_____

_____

_____

_____

_____

_____

_____

_____

_____

PATERNAL:

_____

_____

_____

_____

_____

_____

_____

_____

HOW FAR BACK CAN YOU TRACE YOUR ANCESTORS

MATERNAL

_____

_____

_____

_____

_____

_____

_____

_____

_____

_____

PATERNAL (WILL FOLLOW AFTER MATERNAL TO KEEP IT FROM BECOMING CONFUSING)

WHAT EVENTS WERE HAPPENING IN OUR COUNTRY AT THE TIME THAT YOUR FIRST ANCESTORS CAME TO AMERICA

MATERNAL

_____

_____

_____

_____

_____

WHO WAS PRESIDENT AT THE TIME THAT YOUR ANCESTORS FIRST
CAME TO AMERICA

_____

_____

DO YOU KNOW WHAT BROUGHT YOUR ANCESTORS TO AMERICA

_____

_____

_____

_____

_____

HOW FAR BACK CAN YOU TRACE YOUR ANCESTORS

PATERNAL

_____

_____

_____

_____

_____

_____

_____

_____

_____

_____

WHAT EVENTS WERE HAPPENING IN OUR COUNTRY AT THE TIME THAT YOUR FIRST ANCESTORS CAME TO AMERICA

_____

_____

_____

_____

WHO WAS PRESIDENT AT THE TIME THAT YOUR ANCESTORS FIRST CAME TO AMERICA

_____

_____

DO YOU KNOW WHAT BROUGHT YOUR ANCESTORS TO AMERICA

_____

_____

_____

_____

_____

ANYTHING ADDITIONAL YOU MAY WANT TO ADD

_____

_____

_____

_____

_____

_____

_____

_____

_____

16

FAMILY MEDICAL HISTORY

MEDICAL HISTORY OF FAMILY

MATERNAL

_____

_____

_____

_____

_____

PATERNAL

_____

_____

_____

_____

_____

HAVE YOU HAD ANY SERIOUS ILLNESSES, SURGERIES, OR HOSPITALIZATION

_____

_____

_____

_____

_____

ANY HEALTH ISSUES I HAVE

_____

_____

_____

_____

_____

ANYTHING ADDITIONAL YOU MIGHT LIKE TO ADD

_____

_____

_____

17

JOBS – CAREER

WHAT WAS YOUR FIRST JOB

_____

_____

_____

HOW OLD WERE YOU WHEN YOU FIRST WENT TO WORK

_____

IN YOUR YOUTH, WHAT DID YOU WANT TO BE WHEN YOU GREW UP

_____

_____

_____

IN YOUR TEEN YEARS, WHAT TYPE OF CAREER DID YOU WANT TO HAVE

_____

_____

_____

AS AN ADULT, DID YOU HAVE ANY DREAMS OF WHAT YOU WOULD LIKE TO DO

_____

_____

_____

WERE YOU ABLE TO FULFILL YOUR DREAMS

_____

_____

_____

DIFFERENT JOBS YOU HAVE HAD

_____

_____

_____

_____

_____

_____

DID YOU SERVE IN THE MILITARY; IF SO, WHAT BRANCH

_____

HOW LONG WERE YOU IN THE MILITARY

_____

_____

_____

_____

WHY DID YOU JOIN

_____

_____

_____

RANK AT RETIREMENT

_____

_____

DID YOU SERVE IN ANY WARS

_____

_____

_____

_____

WHERE WERE YOU STATIONED

_____

_____

_____

_____

_____

_____

ANYTHING ADDITIONAL YOU MIGHT LIKE TO ADD

_____

_____

_____

_____

_____

_____

18

MARRIAGE (S)

HOW MANY TIMES HAVE YOU BEEN MARRIED

_____

I MET YOUR FATHER AT

_____

_____

_____

_____

_____

_____

_____

_____

MY FIRST IMPRESSION OF HIM WAS

_____

_____

_____

_____

_____

_____

AT THE TIME WE MET, I WAS _____ YEARS OLD AND HE WAS

_____ YEARS OLD.

WHAT TRAITS DID YOU LOOK FOR IN A SPOUSE

_____

_____

_____

_____

_____

HOW DID HE PROPOSE

_____

_____

_____

_____

_____

_____

WHEN WE MARRIED, I WAS _____ YEARS OLD AND HE WAS

_____ YEARS OLD.

DATE OF WEDDING

_____

WHERE THE WEDDING WAS HELD

_____

WEDDING PARTY

_____

_____

_____

WHAT DID YOU WEAR

_____

WHERE DID YOU GO ON YOUR HONEYMOON

_____

_____

SPECIAL MEMORIES OF YOUR WEDDING

_____

_____

_____

_____

_____

FIRST ADDRESS AS A MARRIED COUPLE (INCLUDE CITY & STATE)

_____

_____

ADJUSTMENTS YOU HAD TO MAKE IN YOUR MARRIAGE

_____

_____

_____

_____

_____

WHERE WERE YOU BOTH WORKING AT THE TIME OF YOUR MARRIAGE

_____

_____

_____

_____

PERHAPS A STEPFATHER HAS BEEN MORE OF A FATHER TO YOUR CHILD THAN HIS/HER OWN FATHER, OR A 2ND HUSBAND (OR OTHER) OF YOURS, THAT HAS HELD AN IMPORTANT ROLE IN HIS/HER LIFE.
IF SO, USE THE SPACE BELOW AND ON THE FOLLOWING PAGES FOR THIS INFORMATION.

I MET MY _____ HUSBAND, YOUR _____ AT

_____

_____

_____

_____

_____

_____

_____

_____

_____

MY FIRST IMPRESSION OF HIM WAS

_____

_____

_____

_____

_____

_____

_____

AT THE TIME WE MET, I WAS _____ YEARS OLD AND HE WAS

_____ YEARS OLD.

HOW DID HE PROPOSE

_____

_____

_____

_____

_____

_____

WHEN WE MARRIED, I WAS _____ YEARS OLD AND HE WAS

_____ YEARS OLD.

DATE OF WEDDING

_____

WHERE THE WEDDING WAS HELD

_____

WEDDING PARTY

_____

_____

_____

WHAT DID YOU WEAR

_____

_____

WHERE DID YOU GO ON YOUR HONEYMOON

_____

_____

SPECIAL MEMORIES OF YOUR WEDDING

_____

_____

_____

_____

_____

_____

FIRST ADDRESS AS A MARRIED COUPLE (INCLUDE CITY & STATE)

_____

_____

ADJUSTMENTS YOU HAD TO MAKE IN YOUR MARRIAGE

_____

_____

_____

_____

WHERE WERE YOU BOTH WORKING AT THE TIME OF YOUR MARRIAGE

_____

_____

_____

_____

ANYTHING ADDITIONAL YOU MIGHT WANT TO ADD

_____

_____

_____

_____

_____

_____

_____

_____

_____

_____

_____

_____

19

MY CHILDREN

NAMES & BIRTHDATES OF MY CHILDREN

_____

_____

_____

_____

_____

THIS BOOK IS WRITTEN ABOUT MOM'S LIFE, BUT HER CHILDREN ARE A LARGE PART OF HER LIFE SO WE WOULD BE REMISS IN NOT INCLUDING A BIT ABOUT THEIR LIVES ALSO.

FOR THE CHILD I AM WRITING THIS BOOK FOR:

STORY OF PREGNANCY, LABOR, AND DELIVERY

_____

_____

_____

_____

_____

_____

_____

_____

_____

_____

_____

YOUR CHILD'S BIRTH WEIGHT & LENGTH

_____

_____

FIRST IMPRESSION OF CHILD

_____

_____

_____

_____

_____

FIRST DAYS WITH YOUR CHILD

_____

_____

_____

_____

_____

YOUR BABY'S FIRST YEAR

_____

_____

_____

_____

_____

_____

_____

_____

_____

SPECIAL MEMORIES OF YOUR CHILD'S YOUTH

_____

_____

_____

_____

_____

_____

_____

_____

_____

SPECIAL MEMORIES OF YOUR CHILD'S TEEN & YOUNG ADULT YEARS

_____

_____

_____

_____

_____

_____

_____

_____

_____

ANY ILLNESSES, SURGERIES, ETC YOUR CHILD HAD

_____

_____

_____

_____

_____

_____

YOUR CHILD & HIS/HER SIBLINGS

_____

_____

_____

_____

_____

_____

WHILE GROWING UP WAS YOUR CHILD INVOLVED IN:
SPORTS, MUSIC, ART, DANCE, SCOUTS, OTHER

_____

_____

_____

_____

_____

_____

MY CHILD WAS RAISED BY:

MOTHER/FATHER   *MOTHER/STEPFATHER*

MOTHER/_____   *MOTHER*

OTHER _____

IF YOUR CHILD HAS BECOME A PARENT, YOUR CHILD AS A PARENT

_____

_____

_____

_____

_____

_____

_____

_____

_____

_____

A FOND MEMORY OF YOU AND YOUR CHILD

_____

_____

_____

_____

_____

_____

_____

AS A MOTHER, I AM THANKFUL FOR

_____

_____

_____

_____

_____

_____

SPECIAL TIMES WITH YOUR GRANDPARENTS

_____

_____

_____

_____

_____

_____

_____

A TIME WITH YOUR CHILD (HAPPY, SAD, SCARY, MEMORABLE...) I'LL NEVER FORGET

_____

_____

_____

_____

_____

_____

_____

PLACES WE LIVED SINCE YOUR BIRTH

_____

_____

_____

_____

_____

_____

HOPES & DREAMS YOU HAVE FOR YOUR CHILD

_____

_____

_____

_____

_____

I AM PROUD OF YOU BECAUSE...

_____

_____

_____

_____

_____

_____

_____

_____

_____

THOUGHTS I WOULD LIKE TO PASS ON TO MY CHILD

_____

_____

_____

_____

_____

_____

_____

_____

20

MY GRANDCHILDREN

HOW DID YOU LEARN YOU WERE GOING TO BE A GRANDMOTHER FOR THE FIRST TIME & YOUR REACTION

_____

_____

_____

_____

_____

_____

NAMES AND BIRTHDATES OF YOUR GRANDCHILDREN

_____

_____

_____

_____

_____

_____

_____

_____

_____

HOW MUCH OF A PART ARE YOU IN THE LIVES OF YOUR GRANDCHILDREN

_____

_____

_____

_____

_____

MY DREAMS AND DESIRES AS A GRANDMOTHER

_____

_____

_____

_____

_____

_____

THINGS I ENJOY DOING WITH MY GRANDCHILDREN

_____

_____

_____

_____

_____

_____

_____

ANYTHING ADDITIONAL YOU WOULD LIKE TO ADD

_____

_____

_____

_____

_____

_____

_____

21

MY ADULT LIFE

WHO DO YOU MOST RESEMBLE IN LOOKS: MOTHER OR FATHER

_____

_____

_____

_____

WHO DO YOU MOST RESEMBLE IN TEMPERAMENT: MOTHER OR FATHER

_____

_____

_____

_____

WHAT IS YOUR POLITICAL AFFILIATION

_____

_____

ARE YOU RELIGIOUS OR SPIRITUAL

_____

_____

WHAT SUBJECTS ARE YOU PASSIONATE ABOUT

_____

_____

_____

_____

DO YOU PLAY A MUSICAL INSTRUMENT; IF SO, WHAT INSTRUMENT

_____

_____

ARE YOU A GOOD SINGER

_____

_____

WHAT DO YOU ENJOY DOING IN YOUR LEISURE TIME

_____

_____

_____

DO YOU SPEAK A 2ND LANGUAGE OR MORE THAN ONE LANGUAGE

_____

_____

A PET PEEVE OF MINE

_____

_____

_____

_____

WHAT ARE YOUR STRONG POINTS

_____

_____

_____

_____

WHAT ARE YOUR WEAK POINTS

_____

_____

_____

_____

I ADMIRE SOMEONE WHO

_____

_____

_____

_____

I LOVE...

_____

_____

_____

_____

_____

_____

_____

WHAT IS THE MOST DARING THING YOU EVER DID

_____

_____

_____

_____

IF YOU COULD MEET ANYONE WHO WOULD IT BE

_____

_____

HAVE YOU EVER MET ANYONE FAMOUS

_____

_____

_____

_____

_____

ANYTHING ADDITIONAL YOU WOULD LIKE TO ADD

_____

_____

_____

_____

_____

_____

_____

22

FAVORITES

MY FAVORITE...

COLOR _____

FLOWER _____

RESTAURANT _____

FOOD _____

BOOK _____

QUOTE _____

PASTIME _____

MY FAVORITE TV SHOW _____

MOVIE _____

SINGER _____

TYPE MUSIC _____

BAND _____

BIBLE VERSE _____

_____

MY DREAM CAR _____

PLACE TO TRAVEL _____

SPORT _____

ANY THING ADDITIONAL YOU WOULD LIKE TO ADD

_____

_____

_____

_____

_____

_____

_____

23

REFLECTIONS ON MY LIFE

WHAT WERE SOME OF YOUR DREAMS OR GOALS:

WORK / CAREER

_____

_____

_____

_____

MARRIAGE

_____

_____

_____

_____

CHILDREN

_____

_____

_____

_____

OTHER

_____

_____

_____

_____

WAS THERE A PLACE YOU ALWAYS WANTED TO TRAVEL, A PLACE YOU
WANTED TO SEE

_____

_____

_____

_____

_____

_____

_____

_____

TODAY IF YOU COULD GO ANYWHERE IN THE WORLD, WHERE WOULD YOU LIKE TO GO

_____

_____

_____

_____

HAVE YOU TRAVELED INTERNATIONALLY

_____

IF SO, WHERE HAVE YOU BEEN

_____

_____

_____

_____

_____

_____

HOW OLD WERE YOU AT THE TIME

_____

_____

_____

_____

WHAT DID YOU LIKE OR NOT LIKE ABOUT YOUR INTERNATIONAL TRAVELS

_____

_____

_____

_____

_____

_____

_____

WHAT WERE YOUR FIRST IMPRESSIONS OF WHERE YOU TRAVELED OUTSIDE THE U.S.

_____

_____

_____

_____

_____

WAS THERE ANYTHING YOU DREAMED OF DOING YOU WERE NEVER
ABLE TO DO

_____

_____

_____

_____

I NEVER THOUGHT I WOULD BE...

_____

_____

_____

_____

_____

_____

_____

ACCOMPLISHMENT YOU ARE MOST PROUD OF

_____

_____

_____

24

DIGGING DEEP IN THE HEART

WHAT MAKES ME HAPPY

_____

_____

_____

_____

_____

_____

_____

_____

WHAT MAKES ME SAD

_____

_____

_____

_____

_____

_____

_____

WHAT MAKES ME CRY

_____

_____

_____

_____

_____

_____

I'D MOST LIKE TO BE REMEMBERED AS A ...

_____

_____

_____

_____

_____

_____

NOW THAT I AM GETTING OLDER, WHAT ONE OF MY BIGGEST
CONCERNS IS

_____

_____

_____

_____

_____

IS THERE SOMETHING MY CHILDREN DON'T KNOW ABOUT ME

_____

_____

_____

_____

_____

_____

25

DEATH & LAST WISHES

WHEN I PASS AWAY, I AM TO BE BURIED AT OR IF YOU DESIRE TO BE CREMATED WHAT WOULD YOU LIKE DONE WITH YOUR REMAINS

_____

_____

_____

_____

IF YOUR MOTHER HAS ALREADY PASSED AWAY, SHE IS BURIED AT

_____

_____

_____

_____

I HAVE LEFT A WILL

YES   _NO_

MY WILL IS LOCATED AT

_____

_____

_____

FUNERAL REQUESTS

_____

_____

_____

_____

_____

WHAT TO DO WITH MY PERSONAL BELONGINGS AFTER I AM GONE

_____

_____

_____

_____

_____

_____

AFTER I AM GONE, PLEASE

_____

_____

_____

_____

_____

_____

_____

_____

_____

DATE OF DEATH

_____

CAUSE OF DEATH

_____

_____

AGE WHEN PASSED AWAY

_____

26

PERSONAL MESSAGE TO MY CHILD

MESSAGE TO MY CHILD

_____

_____

_____

_____

_____

_____

_____

_____

_____

_____

_____

27

ADDITIONAL SPACE FOR NOTES

CONTINUE THE STORY OF YOUR PARENT'S LIFE WITH

'MY FATHER'S LIFE STORY: A DOORWAY INTO MY FATHER'S HEART AND SOUL'

BY

CHERYL PRYOR

www.ingramcontent.com/pod-product-compliance
Lightning Source LLC
Chambersburg PA
CBHW081515040426
42447CB00013B/3230